I0480480

The Art of B2B Sales
- 6C -

"My 26-Years Journey . . ."

DON

ABOUT THE AUTHOR

The author spent 13 years working for major renowned US Multinational Corporation regional offices in Singapore and Malaysia holding the position of Chief Representative, Area Sales Manager, Regional Manager, and General Manager. Thereafter he started a joint venture with major Italian manufacturers for sales of valves, forging, and flanges—handling South East Asia markets for 6 years. It escalated to operating his own SME trading company in Singapore representing manufacturers from Europe, the USA, Japan, Korea & China for the past 7 years.

The author pioneered and built a full-pledged forgings and flanges production facility in Johor, Malaysia together with his joint venture partner and successfully established a distribution network in the Malaysia and Asia region for the operation.

Graduated with an MBA (major in finance), International Business Degree and Diploma in Manufacturing Engineering. The author is a trained engineer with years of knowledge and experience in international business development and financial management.

The author shared his 26-years business journey in the global marketplace. Having represented manufacturers, holding senior positions, and later representing manufacturers as a joint venture partner and independent trading company, he has experienced both sides of the B2B international business.

In the Sales & Marketing of industrial products, markets are relatively more complex, and channels of distribution are relatively shorter. Buyers are well-informed, highly organized, and sophisticated in purchasing techniques; and multiple influencers contribute a different point of view towards the buying decision.

B2B Sales and Marketing involves a high degree of complexity in its decision-making process. Depending on the complexity of the industrial product, the number of parties involved varies. B2B sales can be more complex than B2C and therefore there are various considerations such as customer buying behaviors, the channel of distribution, products' benefits, pricing strategy, product innovation, competition, and after-sales support.

The author originated his 6C factors affecting international business development in B2B, namely: 1st C: Channel to enter a new overseas market, 2nd C: Cost of using these channels, 3rd C: Cultural differences affecting relationship development 4th C: Strategies working with Co-partner, 5th C: Developing Confidence with others and 6th C: Connecting with the world.

He shared his view on the effectiveness of implementing these 6C strategies to apply to B2B sales and marketing in the global marketplace. The author shared his own experiences and stories throughout his past 26 years of working in the Oil, Gas, and Marine industry—his unique encounters with business partners, business associates, colleagues, suppliers, customers, agents, distributors reflecting the realistic international business arena.

TABLE OF CONTENTS

1ˢᵀ C: CHANNEL of Market Entry

What is your strategy for developing international business entering a new overseas market? Depending on the complexity of your industrial product, the market size, market share, after-sales service and support requirement and your budgeted fund allocated, these are the channels that you may consider: (I) Direct Selling (II) Setting up Representative Office (III) Setting up Regional Sales Office (IV) Start own manufacturing facility with Sales Operation (V) Joint Venture with partner to set up Regional Sales Office (VI) Appoint Agent or Distributor. Each of these channels has its own considerations, benefits, and effectiveness towards achieving your desired result.

We shall examine the cost of using each of these channels of market entries in the next chapter. Let us first examine the advantages and disadvantages of using these channels for sales and marketing of industrial products in the B2B environment.

We shall look at the implementation processes and areas of concerns and I will share my own experiences in using these modes of market entries throughout my career.

(I) By DIRECT SELLING

The most direct way of selling industrial products is by direct sales coordinated from the head office via its own sales department. Considering that if you are located 10,000 miles away from your customer, how effective it is going to be in reaching your customer, and what are your chances of closing the deal? Not to forget, the decision-making process for B2B is more complicated than B2C where more parties are involved in the decision-making process. To gain interest in or even to create curiosity about your product by you, each of these different levels of the decision-making process can be a great challenge.

There may be companies who have effectively utilized the latest Artificial Intelligence (AI) technology or IoT (Internet of Things), or direct selling via various E-commerce platforms could also be possible. In most cases—especially where industrial products are complicated or highly engineered—sales through E-commerce or via the internet is not very common at this point in time. This might change in the near future!

We will touch on this topic in the last section of this book (CONNECT). In general, direct selling into a new international market is not a common practice for most B2B global sales. If direct selling is not effective, you may want to explore other options for entering new markets.

(II)   By setting up a REPRESENTATIVE OFFICE

The next mode of entry to entering a new market is by setting up a regional office in the region or targeted market by employing your own sales personnel. Getting the right people is the key to success concerning this option.

First, you must decide if you are going to employ local personnel or send expatriates from your own country or your other regional offices to run this operation. It could also be a mixture of expatriates and local personnel. The most common practice is to send one or two expatriates—those already working with the company from your HQ or other regional offices—to head the operation and employ a few more staff members locally to support him/her.

The greatest challenge then becomes who is the right person to send to that market and how are you going to select the best possible local personnel. Assuming you can get the right team in place, this mode of entry can only be effective if you also incorporate the right incentive plan to motivate the personnel to achieve your desired results.

If you are unable to get the right team in place, this channel can be a disaster instead of a blessing. Instead of bringing in more sales, the wrong team could cost the company a substantial amount of funds (mostly as a fixed cost) and at the same time risk damaging the reputation of the company. These personnel represent the company directly and their operation will impact the company performance directly. Their actions will also directly affect the company's first impression to the new customer.

I have set up a representative office for a major US MNC and was appointed as the chief representative of the operation based in Singapore. I was reporting to my regional director based in Taiwan. My superior visited me twice a year and I went to Taiwan annually for a regional sales meeting and to the USA for an international sales meeting. I was considered a local employee as I have no expatriate benefit, though my salary is relatively good. I employed a secretary and a chemical engineer to assist me in my operation.

We were selling cobalt powder used as catalyst in the refinery. Our sales were stable but there was no real growth. There was no sales training, nor any product training provided for any of the staff in my office. There was no incentive plan for growing the sales nor any career path plan in place.

In fact, my superior felt that my presence in Singapore was threatening his position. Consequently, the better my performance, the bigger a threat it was to him. This structure for operation was not effective, and I decided to leave after one year. The company decided to close the regional office after I left.

If you are considering this option, you need to ensure that there is an adequate motivational and incentive program in place to keep your employees striving for better sales and growth. You must have a good reporting system in place and a good management structure to ensure a clear division of the area of responsibility for each operation and each personnel—to avoid any potential conflict around the operations and avoid any duplication of work.

Keeping in mind that your head office could be 10,000 miles away and your regional office could be 3,000 miles away; it is important to keep these local staff members motivated by implementing the right motivation program inclusive of a monetary incentive plan, and providing an appropriate career growth path.

Getting the right team together—with a good management structure and a reporting system in place with an appropriate incentive plan—can ensure getting the desired results using this mode of market entry.

Simply giving the operation a yearly sales target or exerting more pressure to achieve higher sales, and just leaving these regional offices to work it out by themselves will not work. You may not be achieving the most desirable results, and you may also soon be losing some of your best salespeople that you have initially identified and employed to start the operation.

(III) By setting up a REGIONAL SALES OFFICE

This is one of the common modes of entry into a new overseas market that most MNCs use when selling industrial products. Aside from setting up your own production facility overseas, this is the least costly operation for building your own regional sales team integrating with a good market presence.

The company will establish its own locally registered company and own 100% of the business unit. This is usually set-up as an independent profit business unit. Some companies prefer to set-up as a cost center directly under another business unit within the organization, depending on the management strategic plan. This business unit normally uses some expatriates and some local personnel.

There may be others that decide to use local personnel on a full scale, except for the head of the operation to be an expatriate. Rarely do we see an entire operation using mostly residents. As this is an independent profit center, besides management staff, the company will employ external sales, inside sales, administration, accounting, and finance personnel as well. This involves a substantial amount of investment funds to start; normally it is a major decision by the management should this option be adopted.

This office covers not only the local market; but may also include the entire region such as the Asia Pacific region or South East Asia. This unit brings in sales and should generate adequate profit to justify its existence. Besides sales and profit, this operation is also meant to promote the company's presence in the market or in the region, by providing after-sales support, developing confidence, and creating brand loyalty.

If the market is good and an effective team is in place, this can be a pretty good way of creating a market presence, generating growth in sales and profits, and preparation for further expansion plans in the region. However, if the market turns bad or an ineffective team is in place, this can potentially cost the company substantial loss and drain off the company's funds.

In my 13 years of working with a renowned US MNC regional sales office in the Oil and Gas industry selling valves and related products, I was appointed Sales Engineer, General Manager, and Regional Manager. I was mostly based in Singapore and twice in Kuala Lumpur (Malaysia). I was about to be relocated to Beijing (China); which did not materialize after I decided to leave the company.

I started as a fresh graduate more than 26 years ago working as a Sales Engineer in one of the valve manufacturing companies owned by a family office in the USA. I was selected from a total of 75 applicants. My sincerity and positive attitude won me the job. This was a regional sales office set-up by a reputable valve manufacturer, headquartered in Scotland. Our managing director was a British citizen, while the general manager together with me as sales engineer and a few other inside sales and administration staff were all residents.

Business was good as we were probably one of the only few valve manufacturers with its own regional sales office operating in the region. The competition was very low; the market was good at that time and business was growing exponentially. We generated substantial sales and good profits for the company.

I was promoted to General Manager reporting directly to management in Scotland after both our MD and GM left the company when it was acquired by another US MNC. I continued running the operation and made good sales and profits.

To further support the M&A exercise, this regional sales office in Singapore was instructed by HQ to close the operation and merged with a parent company's regional sales office in Kuala Lumpur (Malaysia) as part of the strategic restructuring exercise.

I was instructed to wind up the operation, retrench all the staff, sell all equipment, and the factory building where we were based. Even though it has been a well-profitable independent business unit generating good sales revenue for the company, top corporate management deemed that it was the best option to merging the two regional sales offices to support the overall growth and merger plan.

One of the main factors gearing towards this decision was the fact that we were sitting on a factory building (land and property) where its value has appreciated 100% over the last 5 years since it was purchased. Simply by selling the factory building, the company could profit US$1 million based on book records.

I was then transferred to the Kuala Lumpur (Malaysia) regional representative office managing the group regional sales for Eastern Asia markets covering China, Korea, Taiwan, and Japan. This operation in Kuala Lumpur was a representative office of the parent company who bought the valve company.

As you can see from my encounters, there are various reasons for establishing the Regional Sales Office and reasons for closing the operation. It could be due to change of the management team, change of management direction, a corporate restructuring plan, merger and acquisition strategic objectives, or potential gain on the value of the asset (as in our case). It could be a combination of these factors.

(IV) By ESTABLISHING OWN FACTORY AND SALES OPERATION

To expand sales into the new overseas market, the company may want to build its own production facility to serve the local market together with the region, in most cases. This could be the most supportive and effective way of penetrating the new overseas market with substantial market presence and giving full support to the customers in the region. This could also be in line with the company's overall strategy of increasing production capability or it could be a strategic reason for reducing the cost of producing the product and gaining benefits through schemes offered by local government to attract investment and transfer of technology.

The reasons vary depending on the top corporate management's overall international business development strategy. In many cases, one of the key reasons for setting up a production facility locally is to serve the local and regional market to gain market share, increase its sales, and to support the customer with good market presence.

Local and regional sales personnel will be set up together with the production facility in most practices. Full administration and engineering personnel may be employed; including inside sales, outside sales, administration, production, accounting, and finance. Considering this is a major investment decision by the company, it involves a substantial amount of new fund injection together with a long-term strategic business plan in place for the operation.

In 2011, my Italian business partner decided to invest in setting up a new manufacturing facility in Asia to produce forgings and flanges. Sales revenue in Asia has grown exponentially in the past 5 years of our operation. To further increase its presence in the market and to provide better support to the customer in the region, my Italian partner decided to set up a production facility to increase their manufacturing capacity and capability to support sales growth in Asia and the Middle East.

Initially, he was planning to set up the factory in China. He engaged a team there to carry out the evaluation to determine the total cost of investment required, and to make appropriate recommendations. Unfortunately, the proposal that he received from the evaluation team was disappointing as they could not tell him exactly what amount of investment was needed. He was given an estimated cost and was told that the amount could increase depending on the obstacles that may arise along the way. He was very upset with the proposal he received and decided to drop the plan to build it in China.

During one of our casual coffee breaks, he was mentioning to me his disappointment of his plan of building a factory in China. I asked him why he was not considering building the factory in Singapore or Malaysia. I was then tasked to do an evaluation for him to determine whether it would be viable to build the factory in Singapore or Malaysia. After much exploring, meeting authorities in both Singapore and Malaysia, further elaboration and consideration, I have recommended building the manufacturing facility in Johor, Malaysia. This decision was based on factors such as cost of land, cost of construction, local government support, taxation, and benefits for local manufacturing offered by government targeted schemes for local investment and technology transfer.

The main consideration between setting up the factory in Singapore or Malaysia was the cost of land and building construction. Building it in Malaysia would cost 30% to 50% of the total cost of building a similar factory in Singapore, all cost included.

Besides, the land in Johor, Malaysia (the place we have chosen) was a piece of freehold land. Which meant that we could own the land and the factory forever. Whereas, industrial land in Singapore (especially for heavy-duty operation such as a forging plant) was a 30-years leasehold. Which meant you only leased the land from the government for 30 years.

The land was purchased, and construction of the factory was completed in 2013. All required governmental approvals to start operations were granted. In addition, I have managed to obtain a Petronas Local Manufacturing License which would give this operation preferential treatment when bidding for local Petronas-owned projects. Petronas is the Malaysian government-owned Oil and Gas producing company.

This operation employed 30 staff; including production, quality control, engineering, administration, accounting, finance, insides sales and outside sales and management. It is currently running in full operation and support sales in Asia as well as Middle East Markets.

One of the key advantages of investing in property and land in Malaysia and Singapore (and most probably also in many countries in South East Asia) is the potential growth of the value of the property asset. The value of this factory that we have built in 2013 (just the land and building itself) has appreciated 100% to 200% over our initial capital investment.

(V) By setting up a JOINT VENTURE SALES OFFICE

Some companies will choose this mode of entering a new overseas market; especially so when they want to gain more market share, increase sales and at the same time create a strong market presence and provide adequate after-sales support to customers. Others may want to use this mode of entry to prepare themselves for a future expansion plan. This is an option where you share the risk and reward of entering a new overseas market by leveraging on your partner's strengths in the new overseas market.

This is an effective way to leverage on another party's presence in the new market and shorten the time it may require to effectively penetrate the market. It can be a joint venture to set up a regional office solely for sales and after-sales support or a joint venture to set up a manufacturing facility or both.

The crucial part of this mode of market entry is to find the right partner, laying out a good joint venture business plan with clear instructions and guidelines, and having a good and fair agreement in place. Developing mutual trust and good ethical business practices will ensure long-term success and growth.

For a joint venture to get started and to avoid any conflict and misunderstanding, these are some initial critical factors that you need to consider and to be agreed upon even before you start the operation:

1) What is the percentage ownership by each party?

2) Who should make the final decision in terms of sales

processes?

3) Which party will take control of all the financials?

4) Who will operate the bank accounts?

5) Who will provide the financing and funding required?

6) Who will provide the initial capital investment or how will it be divided?

7) How should the profit be divided?

8) How should intercompany sales be handled?

In 2007, I was approached by an Italian manufacturer to set up a joint venture regional sales office in Singapore to handle the South East Asia Market. This Italian family-owned MNC has a few manufacturing facilities in Italy, the Middle East and USA. They have an established distribution network in Europe, Scandinavia, the USA, and Middle East.

They have been operating successfully in two or three of the Asia markets, but they believed that much more could be done to further increase the sales in this region. They have tried appointing an agent to handle South East Asia but have not been successful and they were unable to see the results they required. So, they decided to set up a joint venture with a local partner to establish a regional sales office.

I left my job as a regional manager of a major MNC to join this partner to set up the regional sales operation in Singapore. I would hold a minority share while the Italian partner would hold the majority. Initial capital investment for this setup and estimated one-year expenses would be provided by my Italian partner with a paid-up capital of US$ 300,000.

I was given full trust and responsibility to operate all bank accounts and managing the complete operation; including the rental and purchase of new office space, employing new local staff, Profit & Loss and sales operation, including the appointment of new agents and distributors in each of these markets in the region. All required financing and funding would be provided by the bank, guaranteed by the Italy head office.

We generated good sales growth for the company, hitting a sales revenue of US$ 18,000,000 with a net profit of US$ 1,500,000 (per annum) by 2009—within 3 years from the start of the operation.

By that time, we have put in place twelve staff members from the initial setup of only two when we first started. Over the years, we not only generated good profit from our sales operation, but also generated a strong market presence and created brand loyalty. We have also obtained substantial asset value gain on the office properties that we have purchased for our operation.

(VI) By appointing an AGENT

This is one of the most common modes of entry into a new overseas market or even an existing market with the lowest initial cost. Appointing an agent in the market to generate sales can be the most inexpensive channel of selling industrial products. An agent can be appointed on an exclusive basis or a non-exclusive basis. If an agent is appointed on an exclusive basis, all sales generating from that market where the agent is appointed will be handled by the agent.

If an agent was appointed on a non-exclusive basis and multiple agents were appointed, these agents can be divided by the customer segment, industry segment, or whichever division deemed suitable for the industrial product. The principal can also appoint multiple agents by segmenting them based on each individual customer. An exclusive and non-exclusive appointment has its own pros and cons.

From the principal standpoint, if you appoint an agent based on a non-exclusive basis, then the company can decide to go direct, use another agent, or use the appointed agent for every customer or every project or enquiry. This seems to be a good deal for the principal. However, there is always a tradeoff for every option. If the principal decides to appoint multiple agents and make their decision for every enquiry or project, the company will need to engage a full time sales support and management team to focus on handling multiple parties. Depending on the volume of work, this can be a very heavy workload. Lots of support such as sales enquiry, quotation, order processing, technical support, after-sales support, and the managing of these agents will be required. In addition, the principal should not be expecting the agent to put in their full effort to market your product nor creating a good market presence.

If the principal appoints an agent on an exclusive basis, then the agent will spend more time, more resources, and more effort to market your product and promote the sales of your product to the market, creating good market presence and providing good after-sales support to the customers. They will also find various ways of reaching out to more customers and growing sales for long-term business development. However, this will depend on how the principal is supporting the agent in doing their work and in protecting their interest in terms of monetary reward, compensation, and trust. Mutual co-operation and mutual trust are crucial for a successful partnership and generating desired win-win results. I will be touching on this topic in a later section of this book.

Depending on the industrial product segment, the complexity of the product, the market size of the product; the principal normally rewards agents based on a certain percentage of sales as commission. In some cases, the principal will sell to the appointed agent and agents will put on their margin to resell to their customers. In some cases, both options are being used concurrently, on a case by case basis.

As regional manager of a renowned US MNC producing equipment for the Oil and Gas industry, I have appointed many agents in the Asia Pacific region during my 13-year career representing principals and manufacturers. We have adopted exclusive appointments for most of our Asia Pacific markets based on each country or market segment. In some cases, we appointed two or three exclusive agents in each market, segmented by product range.

Each agent would focus on promoting the allocated product range that they have been appointed and would be responsible to generate sales growth and be evaluated based on the segment that they have been assigned. A clear division between agents' areas and responsibilities needed to be carefully laid out and managed to avoid potential conflict and misunderstanding between each party. In our case, some of our agents were inherited by companies that parent companies have acquired over a period. We spent a substantial amount of time managing these agents so that sales and marketing work could be effectively carried out to achieve desired results.

I have been quite successful with my appointed agents in Malaysia, Thailand, Brunei, Indonesia, Taiwan, Korea, and Japan. And we have generated exponential sales growth in these markets. The key to our successful partnership was by developing strong mutual trust and by extending lots of support to them. I would go to the level of ensuring that they receive their commission fairly and timely from our regional offices. I would forward the enquiry which I received directly from a client from their respective allocated market for their handling. I would visit the customer together with them on a regular basis. As I was handling a few markets at one time, I made it a point to visit each country once in every two or three months and at least 4 times a year.

The most important part of appointing an agent is to find the right agent for the market and developing mutual trust and providing strong and sincere support to them to create a successful and long-term business partnership for mutual benefits.

(VII) By appointing a DISTRIBUTOR

This mode of entry is like appointing agents, but in addition, the agent will keep stock of the principal's products for local or regional distribution. Once the appointed agent keeps stock of the principal product, they are considered a distributor.

A distributor can be appointed either on an exclusive or non-exclusive basis. The market can be divided by country, by region/

area, by industry segment, market segment, or product range.

The principal can appoint a distributor for a segment of the industry for a market. For example, a pump manufacturer is appointing a distributor for the Oil and Gas industry in Malaysia. If you are selling products like pumps, it can be used in various industries and various sectors. To appoint one distributor may not be the most effective way. Most distributors focus only on a certain industry or certain sector of that market.

Unless the appointed distributor intends to extend their sales by engaging more sales personnel to ensure adequate coverage, normally each distributor just stays focused on the area in which they are strong. For products such as pumps, after-sales support is very important and can also be a very profitable business unit for the distributor. Besides selling the pump, they can also supply spare parts of the pump and provide product maintenance services to their customers. In this case, the distributor will need to keep stock of the pump and all its related spare parts as well.

After appointing one distributor for the Oil and Gas industry, the principal can then appoint another distributor of pumps for the water industry. Or they can appoint a distributor for the water and wastewater processing industry separately. Depending on the strength of each distributor appointed, the principal can decide on the most effective strategy to segment the market so that they are adequately covered and to maximize the highest potential growth in sales.

In most circumstances where the distributor needs to keep stock—especially so when spare parts stock is also required—the principal will choose to appoint multiple distributors. A clear division of the market for each distributor must be carefully laid out so that there will not be overlap and to avoid conflict and misunderstanding between each party. If this process is not carefully managed, the consequences can be a loss of confidence by each distributor, and they will thus not be motivated to generate sales growth for your product.

If the principal appoints multiple distributors for the same segment of the same market, then the principal needs to ensure that each distributor understands fully how they will operate separately from the other distributors, such as based on the individual customer. Unless the market is so huge that multiple distributors are needed to adequately cover the entire segment, otherwise this mode of duplication is not recommended.

The principal can consider appointing the distributor for each market segment and assist them to expand their business to keep stock in multiple locations to ensure adequate coverage. You can be sure that if it is a profitable business model, the distributor will be more than happy to carry out the expansion plan with you.

You may be thinking that by appointing multiple distributors to keep your stock will create more demand and keep the competition between each distributor; this can be a devastating strategy. Instead of bringing in more sales, the distributor may lose confidence in the principal and none of the distributors will be motivated to push for more sales for you. In a worse case, the distributor may just drop the distributorship after some time realizing the non-viability of the business model, or simply let your product run on its own in the market without putting much effort and resources into their marketing plan.

In the industry where I have been working for the past 26 years

(Oil & Gas), I have seen manufacturers in our industry who have adopted both the strategy of appointing an exclusive distributor as well as appointing multiple distributors; depending on the product range and technical complexity of the product.

Depending on how well the principal is able to segregate each distributor from the other and how well the principal is able to do a proper job of control and support, generally having one distributor for each segment or each market is more effective than having multiple distributors. Especially so when the product is complex and the selling and decision-making process is complicated. The distributor will need to put in substantial resources to their marketing effort and personnel must also be knowledgeable in the product. In some cases, not only sales effort is necessary but also engineers with good technical knowledge of the product are required to provide after-sales support and maintenance services to the customers.

In the industry where I worked, I have seen quite a few successes and a few failures in these modes of entry to a new overseas market. It all depends on how the principal is handling their business partners and the way they have been managed. I have seen a manufacturer from China who uses multiple distributors in Singapore and at the same time also set up their own regional sales office in Singapore. This move created much confusion, not only among the multiple distributors but also with the customers. It resulted in a loss of confidence with all parties involved and ultimately the failure of their marketing effort. The question of business ethics and integrity is a major concern by the end customer as well.

(VIII) SELECTING THE RIGHT PARTNERS

The selection of the right channel partner determines the success or failure of the mode of market entry. Whatever strategy you have adopted means absolutely nothing if the right party cannot be found to execute it. How do you find the right channel partner?

The initial decision for the manufacturer or principal to get the right partner is by making choices based on these considerations:

1) Which are the channels or options available in getting the contact of a suitable partner?

2) Are you looking at an exclusive appointment or multiple agencies?

3) How should the selling function be divided between each agent/distributor and the company sales force?

4) Which portion of the product line shall be sold through this channel?

5) Is there a need to divide the market into different market segments before appointing a distributor/agent?

6) What marketing function are you expecting from each distributor/agent and how they can be divided should multiple distributions be adopted?

7) What policies, guidelines, and specific agreement should be in place to ensure effectiveness, profitable, and mutually beneficial and successfully fulfilling relationships?

8) What desired results are you expecting to achieve from

each appointed distributor/agent?

I will be making some recommendations for your consideration to finding the right partner as your BUSINESS PARTNER in the "Connect" section of this book.

Assuming you have selected the right distributor or agent, they must be managed in such a way that the relationship will flourish into a mutually beneficial result for all parties.

The following factors must be fulfilled:

1. Create distributor/agent loyalty,

2. Train and develop distributor/agent sales and support personnel,

3. Give a realistic target and determine how to evaluate performance against target and to reward accordingly,

4. Distributors/agents should be adequately remunerated,

5. Provide and maintain an effective communication system with every distributor/agent,

6. Show extra support to distributor/agent and sincerity . . . like forwarding of an enquiry to a distributor received directly from the customer.

I will elaborate on the above in the "Co-partner" strategies section of this book.

WHAT'S NEXT:

Due to the limitation of traveling and strict restrictions in place during the current pandemic, it is not easy to put up an overseas representative office or setting up an overseas sales office—at least in the short term until this pandemic is completely over—which may take years.

Building your own production facility and sales operation may not be feasible either. Considering that customers are probably not in the process of adding new suppliers for a while, the most viable and cost-effective mode of entry into a new overseas market at this point of time is to find a right local partner to set up a joint sales office or regional sales office, or to appoint an agent/distributor.

As we move towards the digitalization era, a joint digitization program with your selected overseas partners is inevitable to be part of your next strategic plan towards successful sales growth and long-term development for international business. We shall explore further on this topic in the last section of this book.

"Go to your customer instead of waiting for them to come to you! . . . What are you doing next?

2nd C: COST of Operation

In this section, let us make a comparison on the cost of operation based on each of these modes of market entries that we have identified in the previous section of this book for the sales & marketing of industrial products to penetrate a new overseas market.

Considering the current challenging business environment, prices of industrial products may become very competitive, margins may be squeezed, and businesses could be less profitable. Finding the most cost-effective way to manage your international business development by entering a new market and achieve long-term growth is the key to success.

We shall make a comparison on the different modes of entry into the new market by using a case study to make this illustration.

CASE STUDY: VALVE MANUFACTURER IN HOUSTON

Assuming there was a valve manufacturer located in Houston, Texas (USA) who intend to expand their sales into the Asia Pacific region. This company produces all type of valves for the Oil & Gas Industry, Marine Industry, Refinery Industry, Water Industry. The company employs 95 staff members in HQ with regional offices established in Europe and the Middle East. The company sales revenue for 2019 was US$ 120 million; with net profit before tax US$ 12 million. 50% of sales revenue was coming from the local market (USA), 30% from European countries, the balance of 20% from the Middle East region.

The company is exploring various modes of entry to penetrate the Asia Pacific market and we are to examine the cost comparison based on the identified mode of market entry and the potential sales that could generate from each channel.

o By DIRECT SELLING

The USA is more than 9,000 miles away from your customer in Asia. The valve can be a relatively complex engineering industrial product and therefore selling directly to Asia is going to be a great challenge. Assuming this is the current mode that the company is using to access the Asia market.

The company has established a good website for customers to access information of the company and its products. Two inside sales engineers and one export sales manager have been engaged to fully dedicate to handling the Asia sales. Following are the fixed cost per annum to be considered.

Fixed Cost (per annum):

Two Internal Sales Engineers	US$ 72,000
One Export Sales Manager	US$ 60,000
Traveling Expenses	US$ 30,000

Marketing & Advertisement	US$ 30,000
Exhibition & Promotion	US$ 50,000
Administration & Office	US$50,000
Total Cost:	US$ 292,000

Potential Business Revenue (per annum):

Sales Revenue US$ 3,000,000 – US$ 4,000,000

o By setting up a REPRESENTATIVE OFFICE

Assuming a company is setting up a representative office in Singapore to cover the Asia Pacific region by employing its own sales personnel. The company intends to employ all by using local personnel. Support for quotation and sales processes will be provided from HQ using two inside sales engineers and one export manager.

Fixed Cost (per annum):

Two Sales & Admin	US$ 60,000
One Chief Representative	US$ 80,000
Office Rental (incl. admin)	US$ 35,000
Traveling Expenses	US$ 30,000

Marketing & Advertisement	US$ 20,000
Exhibition & Promotion	US$ 50,000
Two Internal Sales Engineers	US$ 72,000
One Export Sales Manager	US$ 60,000
Administration & Office	US$50,000
Total Cost:	US$ 457,000

If the company intend to send its own personnel from the USA or other offices to be based in Singapore as an expatriate, the above cost should also include the following:

Extra Remuneration for Expatriate   US$ 100,000

Expatriate Housing & Car Allowance   US$ 80,000

Other Allowances   US$ 30,000

Besides the above, the company needs to allocate an additional US$ 50,000 to reward the staff in the representative office for good performance.

Potential Business (per annum):

Sales Revenue   US$ 4,000,000 – US$ 8,000,000

The above is the estimated cost of operating one effective representative office in Singapore. If you are using only one representative office to cover the entire Asia Pacific region, including Australia/New Zealand, and Eastern Asia (Japan,

Korea, China), the coverage may be too wide. We cannot expect the office to deal directly with customers all by themselves. They will need to appoint agents or distributors to cover each country or each segment for individual markets.

o By setting up a REGIONAL SALES OFFICE

Setting up its own regional sales office is one of the most common modes of market entry that many MNCs use when selling industrial products overseas. Aside from setting up its own production facility overseas which involves high investment, this is the less costly operation for international sales operations that offer good market presence.

Assuming a company decided to set up a regional sale office in Singapore to cover the entire Asia Pacific region. It is quite common for the company to send its own management personnel either from HQ or from other regional offices to be based in the new regional office. In this case, we assumed the company is sending 2 expatriates to be based in Singapore for its regional operation as Managing Director and Regional Manager. These are the cost to be considered:

Fixed Cost (per annum):

Two Insides Sales	US$ 60,000
Two Admin Staff	US$ 30,000
Two Account & Finance	US$ 60,000

One Sales Manager	US$ 80,000
Two Expatriates	US$ 240,000
Two Expatriates Housing	US$ 100,000
Two Expatriates Car	US$ 50,000
Two Expatriates Other Allowance	US$ 40,000
Office Rental (incl. all admin)	US$ 80,000
Traveling Expenses	US$ 80,000
Marketing & Advertisement	US$ 40,000
Exhibition & Promotion	US$ 80,000
End of Year Reward for Staff	US$ 100,000
Total Cost:	US$ 1,040,000

Potential Business (per annum):

Sales Revenue   US$ 10,000,000 – US$ 15,000,000

Remark: Support Staff from HQ not included in the above costing.

o BUILD OWN FACTORY AND SALES OPERATION (Based in Johor, Malaysia)

Assuming the company wanted to build its own production locally to serve the local and regional market to gain market share, increase sales, and to support the customer with good market presence. This could be in line with the company's overall strategy of increasing production capability and could also be a strategic reason for reducing the cost of production.

Local and regional sales, administration and management personnel will be set up together with the local production team. Full administration and engineering personnel will be employed; including inside sales, outside sales, administration, engineering, quality control, production, accounting, and finance. Considering this is a major investment decision taken by the company, it will involve a substantial injection of fresh funds and having a long-term development strategy in place.

After a thorough review and evaluation, the company decided to build its factory in Johor, Malaysia on a piece of industrial freehold land purchased from a developer in Malaysia. This developer will also be contracted to construct the building. It will be built on a land space of 2 acres of an industrial estate. Construction costs will include all approvals required from the local government authorities such as a fire safety license, a water and gas license, a safety license, and an electrical license, etc.

Initial Investment:

Land Cost (2 acres of freehold land):	US$ 4,000,000
Building Construction (incl. all licenses)	US$ 3,000,000
Machineries and Equipment	US$ 4,000,000
All other Miscellaneous	US$ 1,000,000
Total	US$ 12,000,000

Fixed Cost (per annum):

Four Insides Sales	US$ 30,000
Four Admin Staff	US$ 20,000
One Sales Manager	US$ 40,000
Three Sales Engineers	US$ 40,000
Three Account & Finance	US$ 50,000
20 Production Staff	US$ 200,000
Four Expatriates	US$ 400,000
Four Expatriates Housing	US$ 70,000
Four Expatriates Car	US$ 50,000
Four Expatriates Other Allowance	US$ 40,000
Administration (incl. bank/finance)	US$ 80,000
Traveling Expenses	US$ 80,000
Marketing & Advertisement	US$ 40,000
Exhibition & Promotion	US$ 80,000
End of Year Reward for Staff	US$ 200,000
Total Cost:	US$ 1,420,000

Potential Business Revenue (per annum):

Sales Revenue   US$ 10,000,000 – US$ 30,000,000

Net Profit before Tax   US$ 1,500,000 – US$ 4,500,000

Remark: Cost of construction and cost of operation in Malaysia is generally 30% to 50% of the cost in Singapore. Industrial land in Singapore is normally on a 30-years lease hold while industrial land in Malaysia is normally on freehold. Labor cost in Malaysia is about 30% to 40% of the cost in Singapore.

Remark: Support Staff from HQ not included in the above costing.

o By JOINT VENTURE REGIONAL SALES OFFICE

Choosing this mode of entry is one of the most cost-effective method and at the same time ensuring business growth together with good market presence. This can be part of the corporate strategy to prepare for further expansion plans in the region. The company will need to decide if they want to hold the majority share of the joint venture or let their local partner take the majority.

Assuming the company decided to set up a joint venture in Singapore with a local partner to handle the sales and marketing for the entire Asia Pacific region. Let us explore the cost of operation for this setup per year.

Fixed Cost (per annum):

Two Insides Sales	US$ 60,000
Two Admin Staff	US$ 30,000
Two Sales Managers	US$ 120,000

One Managing Director	US$ 170,000
Two Account & Finance	US$ 60,000
Office Rental	US$ 80,000
Administration & Financing	US$ 100,000
Traveling Expenses	US$ 50,000
Marketing & Advertisement	US$ 30,000
Exhibition & Promotion	US$ 50,000
End of Year Reward for Staff	US$ 100,000
Total Cost:	US$ 850,000

Potential Business (per annum):

Sales Revenue   US$ 5,000,000 – US$ 10,000,000

Net Profit Before Tax   US$ 500,000 – US$ 1,500,000

o By appointing an AGENT/ DISTRIBUTOR

Appointing an agent by segmenting them into each individual country, each segment, each industry, each region, or each product range is the most common practice in sales of industrial products. An agent can be appointed directly from the head office or appointed from their regional office, representative office, joint venture partner regional office, or its regional production facility responsible for the region/area.

Assuming the company has not set up any of the regional offices nor any joint venture and decided to appoint an agent directly from the head office to handle the Asia Pacific region. These are the cost for consideration operating directly from the head office sales department.

Fixed Cost (per annum):

Three Internal Sales Engineers	US$ 120,000
Three Export Sales Managers	US$ 250,000
Traveling Expenses	US$ 120,000
Marketing & Advertisement	US$ 50,000
Exhibition & Promotion	US$ 80,000
Other Administration	US$ 80,000
Total Cost:	US$ 700,000

Potential Business (per annum):

Sales Revenue   US$ 10,000,000 – $ 15,000,000

Remark: Lots of administration, management, and support activities for agents are needed for this mode of market entry.

A few regional sales personnel are engaged to manage the agents and distributors, and the company can also expect to spend more on traveling expenses and promotional activities.

o SUMMARY OF COST AND POTENTIAL SALES

Mode of Market Entry	Fixed Cost	Potential Sales
Direct Selling (From HQ)	US$ 292,000	US$ 3M to 4M
Representative Office (Singapore)	US$ 457,000	US$ 4M to 8M
Regional Sales Office (Singapore)	US$ 1,040,000	US$ 10M to 15M
Own Factory and Sales Operation (Malaysia)	US$ 1,420,000	US$ 10M to 30M
Joint Venture Regional Sales (Singapore)	US$ 850,000	US$ 5M to 10M
Agent/Distributor (From HQ)	US$ 700,000	US$ 10M to 15M

These costs are meant for comparison purposes only based on a set of assumptions. It does not necessarily reflect the actual cost of operation depending on the size of the operation, the number of resources you are committing into the operation, location of offices, and the number of employees (local/expatriate).

"Go to your customer instead of waiting for them to come to you! . . . What are you doing next?

3ʳᵈ C: CULTURE

Basis of Cultural Differences

Customs, norms, traditions, habits, practices, and even small details like differences in facial expression and body gestures influence the communication process and directly affect the effective function of inter-organization and the interpersonal relationship between organizational parties.

While cultural differences may have only a little effect on the industrial products itself, it does present a major factor towards successful partnership reaping the desired results with direct employees, business partners, business alliances, or clients.

Without obtaining a good understanding of cultural differences of parties involved, it may create potential conflicts and misunderstandings between each party, and ultimately the failure of the partnership or breaking down the business relationship. Cultural miscommunication can be a very costly lesson!

Managing cultural risk by learning how to read and respond to the organizational culture of your overseas employees, business associates, partners, customers, governmental agencies, and regulators is key to building successful and effective partnerships and strategic alliances.

These are some of the considerations on cultural aspects we should examine when handling sales and marketing in B2B:

- Difference in Languages

- Difference in History/Background

- Difference in Business Practices

- Difference in Communication Style

- Difference in Communicating with Employees

- Difference in view on Human Rights Issues

- Difference in handling Governmental Agencies

- Difference in Motivational & Reward Methods

- Difference in Educational System

- Difference in Religion

- Difference in Values on Punctuality and Success

- Difference in Social Responsibility

- Difference in view on Politics

- Difference in Environmental Issues

We will give some illustrations of how some of these cultural differences affect the different channels we intend to use for entering a new overseas market. We will use these cultural differences of different nations, countries, or regions to illustrate their impact on the strategic partnership or alliances, which resulted in the success or failure of the overseas venture.

My personal experiences and unique encounters in this section of the book are meant for illustration purposes. It does not necessarily reflect the actual culture and practices of the nationality as mentioned in this book.

o CASE STUDY 01 – Through DIRECT SELLING

An American company based in Houston clinched a project from a Japanese company based in Tokyo. They decided to fly a team of sales and engineering personnel from Houston to Tokyo for a kickoff meeting. The American company has no local presence in Japan and has no local representative either. They were expecting their Japanese client to be able to understand simple English and therefore did not engage a translator for the meeting.

The American team arrived in Tokyo on Sunday night and scheduled to depart from Tokyo on Friday midnight. Upon arriving in Tokyo, the American team spent Monday to take a short tour of Tokyo city and had a team dinner together on Monday night.

They met their Japanese client on Tuesday morning. Before they started the meeting, the Japanese client conducted a half-day briefing and training on safety and procedure for evacuation as the meeting was held at the site office.

They started the meeting after lunch. After a tiring day, the American team left the client's office late afternoon and had dinner with their own team; followed by a beer drinking session. The American team arrived at the client's office at 9:30 am the next day and ended the meeting at 5 pm and likewise for Thursday.

When the meeting ended at 5 pm on Thursday, they were only halfway through their agenda. Now they needed to change their flight to the following week so that they could finish their discussion on all the outstanding issues. They decided to rebook their flight for the following week Wednesday to ensure having adequate time to finish everything.

Finally, they completed all the discussions with their Japanese client on Tuesday afternoon in time for them to fly back to the USA on Wednesday.

When they reached back to the head office in Houston on Thursday morning, they prepared their Minutes of Meeting and submitted them to the Japanese client, assuming that everything was well and in order. To their surprise, this was the reply they received from their Japanese client, "We have read your Minutes of Meeting. All the points were noted, and we can now discuss how they can be resolved and be carried out"!

The entire American team was furious and upset when they received this message. They thought that all issues were discussed and agreed upon during their five days of meetings in Tokyo. How can the client now say that they need to be resolved and carried out?

They sent a note back to their Japanese client to get clarification. This is the reply, "We have noted all of the issues you have raised during our meetings but we have not come to any agreement as to how they should be resolved and carried out."

Let us examine what are the cultural differences that caused these misunderstandings and failure to establish a good client relationship.

First, during the meeting in Tokyo, their Japanese client kept replying to the American team "Hai" (in Japanese) which means

"Yes" (in English). To the American team, the client has agreed to their proposal. To the Japanese, it meant that I did understand what you were saying; but it does not necessarily mean that I have agreed with your proposal. The Americans kept thinking that their Japanese client has agreed, and they continued pushing on with their agenda without further elaborating and coming to a final agreement.

Second, the meeting which normally takes three days to complete was taking them more than one week. The Japanese are very careful with Safety procedures and therefore spent half a day where the Americans expected to get it done in fifteen minutes.

Japanese are very detailed in all aspects of the work, and they expected their vendor to discuss in detail, and that every small issue should be raised and agreed upon.

Due to the language barrier, even though they could understand each other, it would take a longer time since both parties needed time to digest the information. Therefore, a meeting which normally takes three days took five days to finish. Due to these differences, the Americans' estimated time was totally out from the time required.

Third, after the first day of meetings, the Japanese client would be expecting to have dinner and a drinking session with the American team which apparently did not happen. This may have already created a barrier to developing a good working relationship.

Fourth, the Japanese are expecting the Americans to start the meeting at 8 am in the morning; but it only starts at 9:30 am. From the Japanese culture, even if you had a long drinking session the night before, it does not mean that you should start the next day later.

From my own experience, my Japanese client would arrive at my office punctually and at 8 am sharp for our meeting; even when we had a long drinking session the day before till 2 am in the morning.

From this story, we now know that cultural differences can make a big difference in the outcome of every situation. We need to first recognize that both parties have cultural differences.

We should try to understand the other party's cultural practices and expectations to get ourselves prepared. We would then make all the necessary arrangements to handle these differences.

o CASE STUDY 02 (PERSONAL ENCOUNTER) – in a REPRESENTATIVE OFFICE

I had set up a representative office of a US MNC in Singapore. I am a Singaporean who was employed by a US company. I reported to a Taiwanese superior based in Taipei, Taiwan (Asia Pacific regional office) and parallel reporting to another American superior based in the USA.

My Taiwan superior felt threatened by my existence. He was worried that if our Singapore office performs well, then the HQ may decide to move the Asia Pacific regional office to Singapore, and he may lose job—although my Taiwanese superior did not show it whenever we met. He tried very hard to hide his concern.

However, there were many situations where he had clearly shown his worries.

Our American counterpart did not notice the problem and assumed that everything was going smoothly as planned.

This reflects the cultural differences between all three parties. If they are not handled carefully, the desired result can be devastating.

o CASE STUDY 03 (PERSONAL ENCOUNTER) – in a REGIONAL SALES OFFICE

In the regional sales office of the US MNC where I worked as a regional manager, my regional managing director was an American citizen and he had been working in the USA for his past 30-years career. He had good experience managing the sales distribution channel there.

Coming over to be based in Singapore was his first overseas posting. He could not understand many cultural differences that we Asian practiced—starting from the language we speak to the food we eat.

One day when we were traveling in Malaysia on one of our joint business trips, I stopped over at a roadside store to buy a very delicious fruit which is one of my favorites. It is called "Rambutan".

He was keen to try, so I bought some for him to bring home. Ten minutes after I dropped him back at his house, I received a phone call from him. And he asked "Can you tell me which part of this fruit is edible? When I peeled off the red skin, there is something transparent-like inside and then there is also seed inside this transparent stuff!"

I used to have a colleague from Scotland who loves to eat durian—another tropical fruit here in Asia. In fact, it is known as "King of fruit." If you like it, it smells and tastes good. However, if you do not like it, it smells and tastes terrible.

He once brought some durians home and he knew that his wife and children hate this fruit. He tried to hide it in the kitchen. After a while, his wife was complaining that gas is leaking, and she started looking everywhere in the house to see which pipe the gas was leaking from. This fruit gives off a strong pungent smell. This smell can travel far and if you use your fingers to eat this fruit, the smell will stay on your hand for the rest of the day even if you wash it a couple of times.

Back to my American managing director, since he has been managing the distribution channel for valves in the USA for a long period, he assumed that the same way could be applied in Asia. In the American's distribution practices, stockists keep large quantities of stock in their warehouse and customers could go directly to their warehouse to purchase the valves.

However, in Asia none of the stockists will do this kind of work as no customer will go directly to their warehouse to buy stock. Moreover, each customer's requirement and specification—even for the same size, type and make of valves—could vary.

It took us a long time explaining to him the differences in customer buying behavior and different practices here. This is just to illustrate one of the differences in practice between different regions or continents when it comes to the selling of industrial products.

o CASE STUDY 04 (PERSONAL ENCOUNTER) – during setting up a new FACTORY AND SALES OPERATION

I have set up a new production facility in Johor, Malaysia for an Italian manufacturer to produce forgings and flanges.

When we first decided to purchase the piece of land and reached an agreement for construction of the building with the developer there, my Italian boss asked how payment can be made. To his surprise, the developer asked for a down payment by credit card, which he did. Considering that this was a huge purchase item (involving millions of dollars), down payment for the purchase of the piece of land could be done by credit card charge. Obviously, this is something impossible in Italy. This is uniquely Malaysia!

In this factory, we have employed Malaysians to work as administration, accounting, finance, sales, production, and quality control staff. Most of these production staff members were Malay and some were coming from India. We also had expatriates from Italy.

Due to the differences in cultural practices and religious belief among the employees, a company needs to take these differences into consideration when it comes to management, production planning, and even scheduling. For example, we need to take note that time should be allocated for the Malay Muslim to take their prayer break. Food catering must also be "Halal" for the Malay colleagues. There are also certain words that we should be sensitive about especially when it involves religion.

The challenge of putting together a group of workers coming from different nationalities with different cultures and beliefs was not an easy task. Management would need to first understand their differences and set up guidelines and clear instructions to avoid any conflicts or misunderstandings that might arise.

o CASE STUDY 05 (PERSONAL ENCOUNTER) – in a JOINT VENTURE SALES OFFICE

I have once tried to put two big bosses (one Italian and one Korean) together for a discussion to set up a joint venture for the sales and distribution of their products in Korea. Both were multi-millionaires and both owned huge businesses back home. The deal did not go through and I had been thinking about what went wrong amid the discussion.

After careful thought, one of the factors could be due to differences in practices and culture. The Italian boss was expecting decisions to be made fast and action to be carried out soonest. While the Korean boss was expecting careful planning and thorough evaluation to be carried out before any decision. One was willing to give control to local management while the other was expecting full control of the operation.

These are just some factors that may have contributed to the failure of a successful partnership. However, it does show the importance of managing cultural differences.

I have set up a regional sales office joint venture in 2007 with an

Italian and a Norwegian partner. We have been managing well and our sales revenue hit US$ 18 million with a net profit of US$ 1.5 million in two years from the time of start with an initial investment of US$ 300K. We continued to generate good sales revenue for the next couple of years.

We were invited by our Norwegian partner to go into deeper co-operation by further developing another joint sales and distribution office in Malaysia. We rejected their proposal due to a bad experience we had with them during one of our partnerships in a project.

We have initially agreed on the sharing of profit for a major project that we have taken up together. After we have successfully clinched the project from our client through our months of hard work, our Norwegian partner refused to fulfill the commitment they have agreed upon by claiming on the different interpretation of the wordings of the agreement, by gearing towards their advantage.

The interpretation of the agreement was clearly explained in the beginning during our management meeting in the presence of our regional management team and witnessed by our Italian partner, and have been discussed and agreed upon by all parties involved. However, they have claimed otherwise and insisted that it should be carried out according to their interpretation regardless of what all other parties have interpreted and agreed upon! Clearly, their claim was not reasonable and yet they have persisted without any compromise.

This illustrates the differences in business practices that may cause the failure of a joint venture, partnership, or alliances.

View and perception on the practice of fair business ethics and integrity are critical for every partnership. If one party did not view this as an important part of the business and only focused on short-term gain and the other party viewed otherwise, conflict and misunderstanding would arise, and the partnership would fail.

o CASE STUDY 06 (PERSONAL ENCOUNTER) – when appointing an AGENT/DISTRIBUTOR

Over my year of working as the principal or representative of a manufacturer, I have appointed many agents and distributors in Asia. In fact, the company that I am currently running has been appointed as agent to some of the manufacturers in Europe and Asia. I had interesting encounters with different nations in the process.

When I deal with our German counterpart, they are considered a straightforward party. When they issue their quotation to us, I will not be expecting any further discount. Therefore, I should take those prices as final and not attempt to get a huge discount when I am ready to place the order. I will get into big trouble trying to do it this way.

On the other hand, when I get a quotation from our Italian counterpart, I know that these prices are subject to final negotiation depending on the situation. It does not necessarily mean that they will discount sharply. Depending on the workload in the factory, interest level that they wanted to get the order or their strategic objective of the project, they will handle every deal differently. The discount level can range from 0% to 40%.

When I appointed an agent or distributor in countries such as Indonesia, Thailand, Malaysia, or Vietnam; a major factor for a successful partnership is based on historical relationships and trust between the personnel handling the appointment and the party to be appointed. If the regional manager handling the appointment had a good relationship in the past with the appointed company and the trust has already been established in the past, the chance of a successful partnership is high and there's thus a good chance of getting the desired results for mutual benefits.

If you are a manufacturer trying to appoint an agent in Singapore, then it may be a little different. Singapore companies are more open to working with many parties although past relationships do matter—but not as much as the others. Singapore is a law-abiding country and we show great respect for our law. We will be expecting our partners and counterparts to follow the law strictly.

For countries such as Korea and Japan, they put more value on building long-term relationships. It will take some time to develop trust and mutual understanding. Once the relationship has been established over a period of time, we can expect to develop a long-term, faithful, and lasting business relationship.

I have a renowned manufacturer in Korea (publicly listed in Korea) which extends an unlimited credit limit to me (a relatively small trading company in Singapore) for 90 days when I buy from them. No other suppliers are willing to do this. It shows the trust and support they are willing to extend to their trusted long-term partner.

When I deal with our Chinese counterparts or manufacturers in China, I am looking for parties who are willing to take full responsibility for their services and products. For those parties who refuse to hold full responsibility to their product—especially toward the quality aspect—I will not deal with them.

The Chinese party needs to find ways to ensure its counterpart in other countries feel secure and that they are sincere in holding full responsibility when a product is not matching the requirement.

Understanding the cultural differences and business practices of the appointed agent or distributor will increase the chance of a successful partnership to achieve the desired results.

On the other hand, an appointed agent or distributor should understand the business practices and culture of the principal to

develop a long-lasting business relationship.

WHAT'S NEXT in Corporate Culture:

A common culture will soon be developed into the corporate culture in the new era of business, i.e., moving towards digitalization. Businesses in all nations will be heading in this same direction in one way or another. We need to get our businesses prepared and ready for this game-changer in B2B which already took place in some of the major organizations.

"Go to your customer instead of waiting for them to come to you! . . . What are you doing next?

4th C: Co-Partner

Whichever mode of entry you choose for entering a new overseas market, you must consider factors that will motivate your counterpart, business partners and associates to form a long-term successful business partnership in order to achieve the desired win-win result for all parties.

Let us examine some of these strategies here:

(I)   Comrade Strategy

Your partner should be treated like your comrade going to war with you. In tactically warfare, team building, and teamwork is the key to winning the war. First, you need to discuss warfare strategies with your comrades. Build a detailed strategic war plan. It shall include details such as the number of soldiers to send, the role and responsibility of each soldier, who will be appointed as platoon commander, platoon in-charge, platoon sergeant, and platoon corporal. Preparation work before going to war, etc.

In every war, there need to be sacrifices by each party. Lay down what each party is prepared to contribute and what sacrifices each party is willing to make. These could be the number of soldiers (which are sales personnel), amount of ammunition (which are tools for sales and marketing), training for soldiers (product sales training, product technical training), and funding for the war (which is the investment to be committed).

When entering a warzone, what are the roles that each party will take? Who is going to be on the frontline fighting the war with the enemy (sales personnel facing the customer) and who will be performing the support role, provide backing and backup for the frontline? Who will handle the logistics, preparing the weapons and ammunition, providing rations to the soldiers? (preparation of quotation, technical support, financing, order processing, documentation).

Before going to war, we need to consider what kind of training should be provided, what type of training, and how it should be carried out. Who will provide these trainings?

(Product training, sales training, maintenance training, technical support training, management training).

After the war is won, how should the land and assets seized from the enemy be distributed? (Profit earned to be distributed or how they should be divided).

Once you have laid down all the above, it should be clearly stated; the roles and responsibilities of each party and all the necessary actions to be carried out before the war, during the war, and after the war. This is to ensure that all parties know exactly what they need to do and how it should be done.

As your partner is going to be your comrade, you need to take good care of them. In every situation, their safety is your utmost concern. Make sure that your partner has not been left behind and build your mutual trust along the way. In the army, we say "Leave no man behind!" Therefore, you should ensure that your partner gains your trust through your actions, and you are taking good care of them in every way, and you will not leave them behind.

(II) Loyalty Strategy

To create loyalty and long-lasting relationships, it is important that your partner does not feel or has any perception at any stage that your relationship with them is a temporary one. Every move by you should be viewed as a step forward to building a long-term business relationship.

Nothing is more harmful than having your CEO visiting their territory without calling on them during his trip. Once there is any event that could create uncertainty, it is inevitable that your partner will lose the loyalty that has been developed over a long period of time. Therefore, we need to be very careful, especially if you are entering their territory or their area of work which can be viewed as a sensitive area.

If you have any doubt if your action is causing any issue to your partner, that is already an alarm that you are entering into a sensitive area. Be open to discussion with your partner and be ready to receive suggestions or recommendations from them before you proceed with your action.

Inviting your partner and his family members to join you for dinner is a good way of building loyalty. Showing respect and establishing a good relationship with their family members is important. Do not undermine the power of spouse influence. Most of the time, the husband will consult his wife and the wife will consult her husband when he/she tries to gauge another person's character; especially their business partner.

Organizing visits to factories by your partner's management team or their best performers tend to develop a sense of belonging to the organization. Relationship building between both parties' staff and management team will strengthen loyalty.

Recognizing the success of your partner and celebrating their success together with them will be very motivating for them to do even better for you. Do not be envious of your partner's success or monetary gain from your business. If they can achieve good remuneration return from your business, they will spend more time and effort on your product, and they will be energized to developing a long-lasting and genuine loyalty with you.

(III) Reward Strategy

Developing your partner's full potential in getting the most desirable result for all parties is the key to a successful partnership. Having the right remuneration and reward program for your partner will achieve this objective.

While your partner is being rewarded for their effort, you may be thinking that once your partner is getting more remuneration—especially monetary gain from selling your product—it is going to lower your profit margin. This is a wrong philosophy by any business partner. The more profit and gain your partner can achieve from the venture, the more effort, energy, and investment of time and resources they will commit to your business.

It does not matter how much your partner is able to get out of your business, it is more important to determine how much you can get out of your business or your product. In other words, you just need to focus on maintaining the margin or investment on return you want to achieve from this partnership. Your job is to keep the profit margin or return you want to achieve for your company and leave it to your partner to get the maximum return that he can get from the business.

If they can keep your profit margin and increase your sales volume and yet make lots of money for themselves, this is the best scenario. You should not be envious of your partner if they are making a good profit. If they can grow their business and expand their sales team using the profit they have made from your product, you can be sure that they will allocate even more time and resources to further increase the sales for your product.

Very often manufacturers are afraid that their agent or distributor is making too much profit from their product. They will try many ways to find out the margin that their agent or distributor is making and try every way to lower their margin. And when they found out that their agents are making a good profit, they will try to increase their own prices. Some will even try to reduce the commission payable to their agent from time to time when the business volume increases.

This is such a wrong conventional way of developing international business. Not only will they upset their partner in this way, but they also lose the loyalty that they have taken a long time to develop. This is a strategy of short-term gain by giving up your long-term benefits, which must be avoided.

You should be more worried if your agent/distributor is not

making a profit or not making enough profit from your product. Over time they will start to lose focus and soon they will give up your product or put them into their freezer. In the worst case, they will continue to represent you and yet not doing much for your product. This is the last thing you want for your partnership.

Do not try to create ambiguity with regards to remuneration or reward for your partner. It should be clearly stated in your agreement with them and carefully explained so that all parties involved know exactly what they will be getting at the end of the day.

This will keep everyone motivated to achieving the objectives and goals established by the partnership. Most important is to fulfill the commitment that has been agreed upon when the result has been achieved. Good business ethics and integrity—especially in this area—are so important in developing a long-term and lasting business venture together for further growth.

I have managed several very fruitful agencies and distributorships in my career. There were many situations where I had to convince my top management of the importance of fulfilling our commitments to the agent such as timely payments of agreed commissions, and never to reduce or change the allocated commission during the time of payment. This is a very important business ethic that in principle must not be compromised. Over time I have gained good trust and reputation from all my agents and have developed very successful partnerships generating good sales growth for our company.

(IV) Development Strategy

Provide training and development of the sales and marketing team members, be it your own sales team or your partner's team. This will ensure that your frontline sales personnel can perform a more effective job. Half the battle is lost if you have non-competent sales personnel. If they do not know the product well and are unable to give a good presentation of the product, the customer will lose confidence and company credential is seriously affected.

Sales and marketing personnel should be trained thoroughly on the features and benefits of your product and understanding the buying behavior of each level of the decision-making process, and the way to handle each of them. Selling skills, communication skills, presentation skills, and negotiation skills are all essential for effective sales personnel.

If you do not train your sales personnel before sending them to the customer, it is similar to sending your soldiers to fight the war without giving them any weapons or ammunition.

Engineering and after-sales support or maintenance training should be provided for the after-sales support team. Especially for industrial products that require servicing or maintenance. It is essential that local personnel must be trained to handle this aspect of after-sales support. It is difficult to convince your client that they can depend on you for after-sales support if you do not have qualified technical personnel locally ready to help them in times of need.

(V) Performance Evaluation Strategy

Depending on the performance of the party you are evaluating; different sets of results should be laid out for direct selling sales personnel, the representative office, joint venture office, and regional sales office. These are some of the standards of performance you can consider:

- Sales Volume
- Market Share
- Number of Active accounts
- Growth Objective (percentage sales increase)
- Inventory Turnover (for distributor)
- Profit (for joint venture/regional sales office)

Besides direct employee sales personnel, most of these parties do not work directly for your company and therefore should be treated with considerable tact and diplomacy.

What constitutes a good performance may not necessarily be the same to your counterpart and overseas partners. Therefore, these measurement standards must be jointly discussed and agreed upon by all parties. Setting standards that are neither realistic nor achievable can do more harm than good. Standards must be meaningful in the sense that all parties should be aware of their role in meeting these set goals. It should not be too complicated and could be measured on a quantitative term.

Such an evaluation should be carried out at periodic intervals (quarterly, half-yearly or yearly) and results should be discussed jointly. It should include identifying weaknesses, industry trends moving forward and strategies to adopt for the next course of action.

Evaluation methods must be based on standards that are directly related to the relevant industry standard and measurable. Evaluation forms can be set up for all sales personnel and issued to them in the beginning so that they understand exactly how they will be evaluated at the end of the day.

(VI) Communication Strategy

Maintaining an effective mode of communication between all parties is an essential part of developing a successful partnership. Very often conflict and misunderstanding arise due to poor communication.

Due to cultural differences and language barriers, communication through email messages or telephone can sometimes create unnecessary misunderstandings. This mode of communication cannot clearly show the facial expression or body gesture expressing the correct message to the other party. Different parties having differences in cultural backgrounds can perceive the same message differently.

In the current high-tech era, it is highly recommended to use video calls if meeting in person is not possible. A video conferencing app such as Zoom, Skype, or Google Meet can be used. This will be more effective than email or telephone if sensitive issues or important topics are to be discussed.

Effective communication channels should be established between all parties. It must be clearly stated as to who in your organization will be responsible to communicate with the other party. It should be more than one person in your organization in case the first person responsible is on leave or not available.

The person responsible to communicate with the other party must always promptly respond to any messages received. Keeping the other party in suspense by not replying to their message is a bad communication skill. If the information requested is not available, you can reply by asking the other party to wait for your response to their query. Communication breakdown is the last thing you want for any partnership.

I remember there was a time when I was working in the US MNC regional sales office where my managing director is an American expatriate who just arrived from the USA to be based in Singapore. He called me into his office one morning and requested for me to become his interpreter. He was having a discussion with one of our local colleagues.

I was confused as both were communicating in English. After listening for a while to their conversation, I realized that my local colleague was using our local English, which we call "Singlish." It could include English together with some mixture of local Chinese dialects and some time with a little Malay language. For an American who has just arrived in Singapore for the first time, it is inevitable that he will find it difficult to completely understand this unique language only used by Singaporeans.

My managing director has done the right thing. Having another person to explain to him and ensuring that the message was correctly interpreted to avoid any misunderstandings was a wise move.

In the event, of you not being sure your message can be correctly interpreted—especially where both parties are using different languages—it is highly recommended to use a third party to translate the message correctly. Clarity in communication is crucial in developing a long-term and trustworthy business partner or associate.

There are many digital communication tools we can use today in the IoT era such as Facebook, Instagram, LinkedIn, or Website to promote your product or to provide information to your partners and the public. We shall discuss this in more detail in the "Connect" section of this book.

"Go to your customer instead of waiting for them to come to you! . . . What are you doing next?

5th C: CONFIDENCE

Establishing a good reputation and gaining the confidence of your company and your company's products are critical factors in gaining access to a new overseas market. Having a consistently good quality product, providing after-sales support for your product, giving reassurance, developing trust, and having good testimonies by users are the path towards building brand loyalty and long-term customers.

Let us review some of these factors here.

(I) Perception of a company

In building confidence in your company and your company's products by your customers or your potential partners, you should first establish a good perception of your company. This is the initial step to create curiosity about your product.

Besides having a good product which could offer many benefits to your customer, you will have to create brand awareness and product curiosity.

There are a few traditional channels of creating curiosity. You can participate in trade shows, participate in related industry conferences, advertise in an industry magazine or on a public TV program. However, these channels could be outdated soon in the "New Normal" business era after the pandemic.

You should start exploring multi-media digital communication channels on the Internet such as Facebook, Instagram, LinkedIn, Google, Alibaba, Amazon, etc. Most communication in the near future will be done via IoT.

Traditional communication channels may be phased out soon. As most people will be using mobile phones and the internet to access information, we need to fully explore the fullest potential of digitalization to send information to your targeted audience. We will explore further on these channels in the next section of this book.

One of the most effective methods of promoting your company or your company's product is to produce a short video clip. This can be broadcasted in the multi-media digital channels which can be accessed by phone and laptop. Typically, these clips should be less than one minute. The attention span on mobile advertisement is very short. If your video clip is more than one minute, it will not be as effective.

To engage professionals to come up with good ideas and interesting copywriting to make it more interesting and more engaging. The cost of doing this is relatively inexpensive now. In fact, you could even try producing it all by your own team.

It is very important how your customer will perceive your company and its products. Here I would like to share with you my personal experience.

I have come across a few European manufacturers who managed to portray themselves to look like a big company where the actual size of their manufacturing facility is relatively small. Once they have gained this perception and trust from their potential customers—and they ultimately could produce the expected quality to meet customer requirements—they have already successfully secured another new customer.

On the other hand, I have also seen a few manufacturers from China where they have a big manufacturing facility and could produce a relatively good quality product, and yet they were unable to portray themselves effectively and sufficiently to the public. I have visited one such company in China.

When I saw the way how they presented themselves in exhibition and the brochure I have received from them, I would have thought that they are a small manufacturer. However, when I visited their factory, I was completely amazed. They had such a big manufacturing facility that I could hardly see the other end of the building. They were using one of the most advanced equipment you could find in the industry, together with a relatively good quality control system in place. However, they were unable to portray the right perception to their potential customers and reflecting their real strength, and were thus unable to attract the rightful curiosity.

Therefore, having your potential client have a good perception of the company is the first step to creating curiosity, and could ultimately be securing another new customer for you.

(II) Quality of a Product

Having a good product which offers many benefits is the first step. Having a strict quality system in place to ensure that your product's quality level is good is a critical factor in gaining your customer's confidence in you.

The next most important step is to ensure that the quality of your product is consistently good. Supplying a consistently good quality product to your customer will build up the trust and confidence in you and ultimately towards developing another repeat customer.

I once bought a huge number of flanges and fittings from a supplier in China to supply to a refinery project in Vietnam. The quality level of this first lot of orders I had with this supplier was good. We then placed a larger second order with them. However, when the second lot of items arrived on site, the quality was so poor and unacceptable that our customer rejected the entire lot of shipment.

I immediately flew to the site in Vietnam to inspect these materials after I received the complaint from the customer. I was shocked that the quality of the second lot of items were totally different from the first lot. I decided to replace all items for my customer by purchasing stock items from distributors in Singapore in order not to cause further delay to my customer's schedule. By doing so, I incurred a loss of more than US$ 100,000.

We claimed our loss from this supplier in China. They refused to accept our claim by giving all kinds of excuses. That was the last order we placed with this vendor. They have lost a customer which took them a long time to develop and secure and they simply lost it in just one order by not taking full responsibility for the quality of their product.

On the other hand, I was willing to hold full responsibility to my customer in Vietnam by replacing an entire lot of material with even more expensive stock items and airfreighting them to Vietnam to expedite the replacement process.

By doing so, I have gained strong confidence and trust from this customer. This happened seven years ago. Up till today, this customer has repeatedly been coming back to me on every one of their projects and, in fact, becoming one of my main customers.

The credibility of your company will be lost if you are unable to produce a consistently good quality product. Even worse is if you refused to hold full responsibility for the quality of your product. However, if you could supply consistently good quality products and are willing to hold a strong commitment for its quality, you have a good chance of building a long-lasting repeat customer.

(III) After-Sales Support

After-sales support is a necessary pillar for industrial products. Depending on the mode of entry you have chosen to enter a new market, this function is a necessity to build customer's confidence. This is especially so if your product needs regular maintenance for it to last for a long period of time.

If a maintenance program is needed for your product, you should carefully consider the right mode of entry to your new overseas market. Direct selling or just setting up a representative office—by not having any presence in the market—may not be an option. You will need to consider the remaining options such as regional sales and a servicing office, joint venture, or appointment of an agent or distributor.

These modes of entries must include a product servicing department equipped with trained product maintenance personnel to handle the after-sales market. If this after-sales support department is strategically implemented, it could be a good profit-generating business unit as well.

I have seen several manufacturers making more profit from their after-sales market than the product itself. Their profit margin on the spare part was much higher than the profit margin on the product. There were other companies that adopted the strategy of selling their product at cost and only making a profit from their maintenance or servicing program or by selling their spare parts at a much higher margin.

In most circumstances, customers will tend to use your servicing team and buying your spare part if the original product was coming from your company. In some cases, there was also concern that the warranty of the purchased product may become void if the original spare parts were not coming from the same company or the same brand creating long-lasting brand loyalty.

(IV) Provide Reassurance

Consider how you can offer reassurance to your customer or your partners to gain deeper confidence in your company. For example, when handling your overseas business partner, you can consider putting certain commitments in your agreement with them to ensure that you will hold full responsibility to the quality of the product supplied.

Undertaking to take full responsibility for the quality of the supplied product and to make replacements totally at your own cost, and compensating them for their loss, will indicate a strong commitment and show the strong confidence of your product quality.

You must show them through your actions; not simply by committing verbally without fulfilling your commitment. Once you have shown your partner that you are strongly committed to your promise, you are on your way to developing a long-lasting relationship.

I have a supplier from China who has been supplying products to me for the last three years. There was once a huge quantity of pipes delivered to me in Singapore for one of my shipyard segment customers. Thirty percent of these pipes failed the quality check by my customer's quality control department.

This Chinese vendor took full responsibility by working with me to quickly replace all the failed pipes. We worked together to find replacement pipes from stockists in China and Singapore. In total, we incurred a loss of US$ 120,000. This vendor even flew over to Singapore to assist me in resolving the issue with my customer. After which they deducted the full amount of our loss from their invoice to me.

I continued to work with this vendor on the next few projects and, in fact, they are currently my main vendor from China. I have placed many good orders to them after the incident and they are my exclusive business partner for China source.

(V) Developing Trust

Building mutual trust is a key factor in establishing a successful partnership. In handling your business partners (Joint-Venture or Agent/Distributor) or overseas employees (in the regional office), you must first build up mutual trust. For others to trust in you, you must first trust them to start. If you cannot trust your partners or the staff that you employed, it is better that you do not use them at all. If you want to work with them, you have got to trust them. Otherwise, the relationship is not going to work.

Once they know that you trust them, they will be motivated to work with you. On the other hand, if you try to hide information from them or try to do things behind their back, the relationship will collapse in a matter of time.

In my career, I have met different groups of business partners. They could be my agents, my distributors, my employees, my shareholders, my directors, my vendors or suppliers, or my joint-venture partners. Those that managed to build mutual trust always ended with a very successful partnership and those that lost mutual trust often ended up with failure.

I am very fortunate to have an Italian business partner that had trust in me to start a regional sales office with him. Though he provided the full investment fund to start the operation, he trusted me to run the entire operation on my own, including full control of all financials and bank accounts. He provided full financial support and operational support from HQ.

He has taught me many valuable lessons in running a successful business. In turn, I provided him with full financial reports on a periodical basis—thus creating mutual trust and understanding between both parties. We generated a continual six years of growth and good profit for the venture.

(VI) Testimony

The most effective way of developing trust and confidence is to provide testimony by your current customers, suppliers, partners, business associates, or employees. Sharing with others these testimonies of their positive experiences dealing with you or your company can be a very convincing strategy.

It is highly recommended that these testimonies be recorded either in writing or in a video clip showcasing their good experiences dealing with you. These materials could be used on your website, brochure, exhibit, digital media, or multi-media.

Your potential partner, business associate, or customer could get references from others (especially reputable persons) to build confidence in starting a new business relationship with you.

Showing testimony recorded of your business associates and clients' experiences with your product and your company may not be a common practice in the B2B environment. However, industry players should start trying it in this new business era. You are going to see the effectiveness once you have tried it. Take the first step and experience it for yourself.

Multi digital media is the upcoming trend and should be used effectively by fully utilizing Artificial Intelligence to further enhance the communication flow and ultimately reflecting a real positive message to your targeted audience. It can be one of the most effective channels of communication with the lowest cost as compared to other traditional methods such as exhibitions, conferences, or brochures if you explore its fullest potentials.

"Go to your customer instead of waiting for them to come to you! . . . What are you doing next?

6th C - CONNECT

Digital Marketing Phases

In the current ever-changing global business environment, digital marketing for B2B is the upcoming trend and growth area. Recognizing the need to start a digital marketing department will be a good start. Engaging a professional in this area to assist your company in its digital marketing effort will become an essential part of your company's global marketing program.

Traditional methods of marketing may continue in the short term, but it will gradually be phased out by digital marketing in the near future. Whichever mode of entry you have selected to enter a new overseas market, digital marketing will complement its global marketing effort and will greatly assist your overseas partners in its local marketing program.

Integrating online marketing into your overall marketing strategy is going to be the "New Normal" in B2B. There is an urgent need to leverage on online customer acquisition and engagement strategies into your global digital marketing implementation plan.

Successful digital marketing must go through these phases of building curiosity, building trust, followed by conversion, and monetization to achieve the desired result.

(I)   Build Curiosity

You may start by using customer engagement channels to connect with the customer. A video clip is one of the most effective modes of building curiosity. It can be published and broadcasted in these digital customer engagement and customer acquisition channels.

Some of the "CUSTOMER ENGAGEMENT CHANNELS"

shutterstock.com • 542262367

- ✄ Social Networking Sites: LinkedIn, Twitter, Facebook
- ✄ Photo/Video Sharing Sites: YouTube, Flickr, Instagram
- ✄ Blogs/Website
- ✄ Mobile Apps

Customer Acquisition Channels:

- Email
- Search Engine Optimization
- Paid Search
- Online Paid Advertisement

(II) Build Trust

Once you have attracted your customers' attention, you can lead them to your Web Landing Page, which could be your Webpage, website, Internet home page, or online ecommerce site. This site can be displaying your video clip or banner showcasing your product or your company; whichever material that could start to build their trust in you.

It can also be showing testimonies of your current customers, suppliers, business associates, and employees of their good experiences with your product and your company.

(III) Build Conversion

Within your Web Landing page, there should be a connection to attract the customer into a commitment page. It can be directing them to register their personal contact details for your sales personnel to follow up, to go into your ecommerce site for making purchases or a further commitment or expression of interest to connect with you.

(IV) Build Monetization

If you have an online store, you can monetize by having your customer make their purchase online. If you do not have an online ecommerce store, it may be time for you to explore further in this area. If you want to start an effective online store in the shortest time with the least cost, there are several online platforms you can explore. You may tie-up with a host to leverage on each other strengths.

Online ecommerce will soon be commonly used for the sales and marketing of industrial products. It is only a matter of time that most businesses will incorporate online sales and online marketing into their international business development plan. The soonest you get started, the better your position will be in preparing for the future buying pattern of industrial buyers.

I have established a new startup, an online ecommerce trading portal for buying and selling of industrial products. You may access my website at: **www.eogplatform.com** for more details.

At this time, my ecommerce platform is meant for the trading of valves, pipes, fittings, and flanges for the Energy Industry. I have more than 30 stockists with strategic alliances with me to list their products online for sales on my website. This platform is highly scalable. It can be extended for sales of other industrial products in other industries with modification.

This is going to be the upcoming trend for the sales and marketing of industrial products going forward. B2B transactions will gradually move towards digitalization mode. As international traveling in the short term is going to be limited due to the post-pandemic "New Normal," global marketing development through digital means is the solution. The earlier you get started on these programs, the better prepared your team will be in implementing a digital international business development plan.

(V) Build Result

Once you get your customer to connect with you online, be it via an ecommerce platform or via a Web Page—giving you more information about themselves—you can then make full use of these data to further your marketing development using AI (Artificial Intelligence) and IoT technology. Having customer data and working through their buying behaviors, you can abstract much valuable information for your sales and marketing development effort and to further incorporate them into your Research and Development program. AI can also track your potential customers and aggressively follow up with them through your marketing program.

This information can be incorporated into your future digital global marketing program; especially useful when introducing new products or developing a new marketing strategy. It can also be another effective channel for scouting for potential business partners or agents/distributors in a new overseas market.

Start evaluating your operations and determine what will be the game changers to impact your international marketing effort and make preparation for your next phase of industrialization using Artificial Intelligence via Digitalization. There are many amazing digital marketing tools already in the market where you can advance your marketing technology that allows you to identify, reach, and engage your targeted audiences better, faster, and more cost-effectively.

Upcoming Trend towards Digitalization in Sales & Marketing of Global B2B

o **Exhibition & Conference**

The conventional method of participating in exhibitions and conferences to promote your products may not be viable anymore—at least in the short-term period. Within the next 6 to 12 months, traveling overseas will be limited and gathering of big crowds will be avoided. The organizing of most exhibitions and conferences will be canceled or postponed.

The alternative to traditional exhibitions and conferences will then be via digital or virtual mode. Virtual exhibitions and Web-based conferences can be rolled out. The organizer can start their online digital exhibition via a virtual basis.

Industry-based exhibitions can host virtual booths for rental. They can create a web-based host for a virtual exhibition for a scheduled period (like the traditional method—a few days or a week). An online marketing implementation plan can be carried out by the organizer to create curiosity, trust, conversion, monetization, and thus resulting in interested parties registering to participate as exhibitors and visitors.

Each exhibitor can create a virtual booth to exhibit their products. This could include video clips and 3D-modeling. Video recordings could be about the products and services or even testimonies from current users or business associates. It could also be linked to a live Web meeting online (face-to-face) or via live webinar. All media of communications shall be digitized and uploaded on the organizer's hosting web.

The host shall reorganize all data and information received from all exhibitors and reorganize and segment them into different groups and categories for ease of access by visitors. There shall be scheduled Web-based conferences conducted via live webinar within the virtual exhibition period. Live virtual conferences shall be the "New Normal" in this business era.

o Visit & Meeting

Live face-to-face meetings via mobile application (Zoom, Skype, Google Meet) will soon be used for most meetings with customers and business associates. An introduction meeting, product presentation, kick-off meeting, management meeting—all these meetings can be conducted via video conferencing through these mobile apps.

Due to the COVID-19 pandemic, everyone is forced to work from home and unable to travel—even travel on land to visit local customers are avoided. Video conferencing becoming the only alternative to communicate face to face with the other party. After the pandemic is over, this mode of communication will continue to be used and, in fact, is going to be the "New Normal" in all B2B communication.

Whether you like it or not, video conferencing could be a necessity to build up your relationship with your customer. It may not be too comfortable to meet in person for quite some time. Sales personnel must start to get used to this mode of communication, or they may be lacking behind in doing an effective sales and marketing job.

o Scouting for a Business Partner

To look for a potential joint venture partner, an agent, distributor, supplier, principal, or candidate for a representative office can be a challenging task—at least for a short-term period. How do you then go about the search process to find the right one? Just like employing new staff, engaging a professional headhunter will probably get you good candidates, engaging a professional third party could be one way of doing it. However, this could be a costly method.

Another effective way is to get leads to potential partners from your potential customer overseas. If you already have a customer in that market, try to find out which suppliers are currently servicing them on similar or related products. The company may not necessarily be selling the same type of product or else they may already be representing your competitor.

It could be another vendor servicing the same customer but selling different products. This is just the first step—after which you will need to conduct your own evaluation and further discussion. As mentioned previously, building a successful partnership involves creating mutual trust and co-operation incorporating all the factors we have discussed.

Introduction or recommendation by another trusted industry peer could be one of the most common practices. Depending on the party that is making the introduction to you and together with other factors of consideration, this may or may not necessarily be the best candidate.

Another mode of search for potential partners and candidates is via online networking. It is going to be the upcoming trend of connecting with customers and industry peers. Scouting for potential customers, business associates, suppliers, partners, and even candidates for employment can be done via online networking.

Each industry could organize their own networking via social networking websites (e.g., Facebook, Instagram, LinkedIn). Most industry players have already started their own live events using webinars. There will soon be various B2B industry hosts that could connect industry players, where manufacturers could connect with potential partners, agents/distributors, and suppliers. And these interested parties could also connect with potential manufacturers or principals via these networking programs.

I am organizing a B2B global connection networking site using my own newly created engagement webpage. Besides networking with industry peers, I may be conducting discussions via webinar on the latest trends and developments in the B2B Global Marketplace. If you are keen to be part of my exercise, you are most welcome to register yourself there. A link will be provided in my Final Statement of this book.

"Go to your customer instead of waiting for them to come to you! . . . What are you doing next?

Final Statement

I thank God for this opportunity to reflect upon my 26-years journey in international business development where I can put on record my past experiences and thoughts. I hope this book will be beneficial to you and that you will find it interesting to read and gain a little extra knowledge in your business journey.

I have shared my experiences and unique encounters with business friends from different walks of life, with different nationalities, different cultures, different backgrounds that I have met throughout my career. I am blessed to having the opportunity to be part of every mode of channel that businesses use to enter a new international market.

I was appointed chief representative of a US international corporation, I worked in a regional sales office of a renowned US MNC, I was in a joint venture with a large Italian family-owned conglomerate, I pioneered in building a new manufacturing facility in Malaysia jointly with my Italian partner, I started a new IoT startup and I am currently running my own trading business in the Oil and Gas industry.

In all these ventures, I have encountered various difficult situations, faced many obstacles, and overcame many challenges, and experienced several high and low moments. I have learned valuable lessons throughout the journey in every aspect of business along the way. I have met different types of businessmen and learned great lessons from them.

My sharing involved my special encounters with people from Japan, Korea, Taiwan, China, Indonesia, Thailand, Malaysia, America, Italy, Germany, and other nationalities. Some were positive experiences, whereas some were not. Both provided me with good lessons where I have learned to use it to improve myself.

In most circumstances and most nations, they tend to have good people who demonstrate good business ethics and good integrity and are always willing to help others. And on the other hand, we do have those that do exactly the opposite. Therefore, my unique encounter with people from each nationality does not necessarily reflect the usual business practice and culture of that nation.

I have shared my learning experiences through my 6C journey in B2B international business development with regards to the Channel of entering a new international market, Cost of each of these channels, Cultural differences of different nations, soldiering together with a Co-partner, business associates and partners like comrade battling together in a warzone, creating Confidence in you and your company and lastly, the latest trend in Connecting with the business world.

And finally, recognizing that Digitalization is the upcoming trend that is going to be the key for B2B transactions and in engaging with your customers. Therefore, examine how you are going to reach your customer instead of expecting them to come to you!

I hope my book will be a good learning experience for you on your journey to the B2B international business arena.

I am setting up a new industry networking webpage to assist

those who want to connect with potential business associates and partners overseas. I will be listing down the different industry groups and you may be invited to indicate your interest area so that I could connect you with those interested parties sharing your goal and objective when you register on my webpage.

I may be organizing a webinar to conduct live conferences or discussion groups and other live events to discuss upcoming trends. I strongly encourage you to register with me on the following link to keep informed and updated.

If you like to hear more stories about my business encounters, my further sharing of my next chapter of business journey or you may have questions to ask me, you can contact me on the following link.

B2B Networking Registration Link (Free of Charge): **www.6cstrategy.com** *Only Name and Email required.*

Please register to stay connected with our networking community!

My Facebook: **www.facebook.com/don.tan.12979**

Please follow me on my FB account. I look forward to meeting you there!

My Linkedin: **www.linkedin.com/in/don-dt-958406103**

Please follow me on my Linkedin account. You can receive my latest update!

Thank you!

"All the glory and honor to our Lord, Jesus Christ!"

www.ingramcontent.com/pod-product-compliance
Lightning Source LLC
Chambersburg PA
CBHW020601220526
45463CB00006B/2398